THE
ENNEAGRAM
TYPE 7
journal

A Guide to Inner Work & Self-Discovery
for The Enthusiast

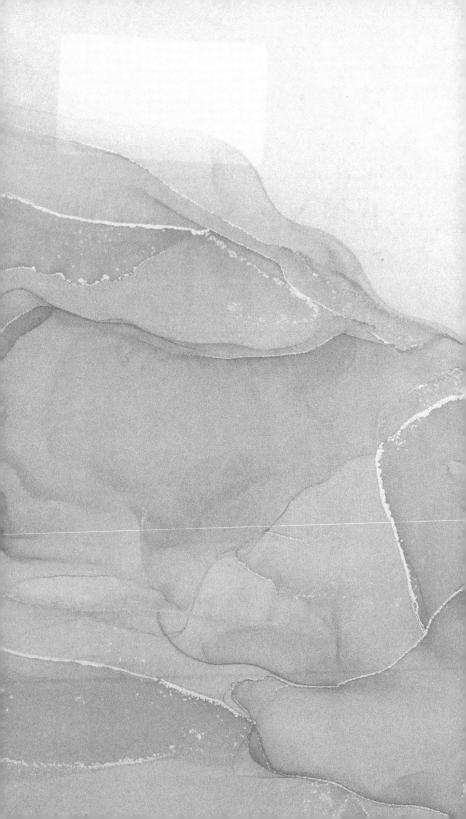

THIS JOURNAL BELONGS TO:

_____

THE
ENNEAGRAM
TYPE 7
journal

DEBORAH THREADGILL EGERTON, Ph.D.
& LISI MOHANDESSI

HAY HOUSE LLC
Carlsbad, California • New York City
London • Sydney • New Delhi

This journal is dedicated to
Margaret Givan Threadgill,
who filled my days with sunshine
and my nights with stars.
Your strength and resilience
continue to transform every
chapter of my life.

You are gifted with a body that allows you to be here in the present moment, a mind that opens access to unlimited possibilities to be explored, and a heart that holds the enormous capacity to love and be loved.

This is the authentic you. You will find yourself when you accept the beauty of your true nature.

Gratitude for who you are is the first step.

Grace will follow.

Caritas,
Deborah & Lisi

CONTENTS

*Enjoy your journey, and
may you find love and
light within yourself.*

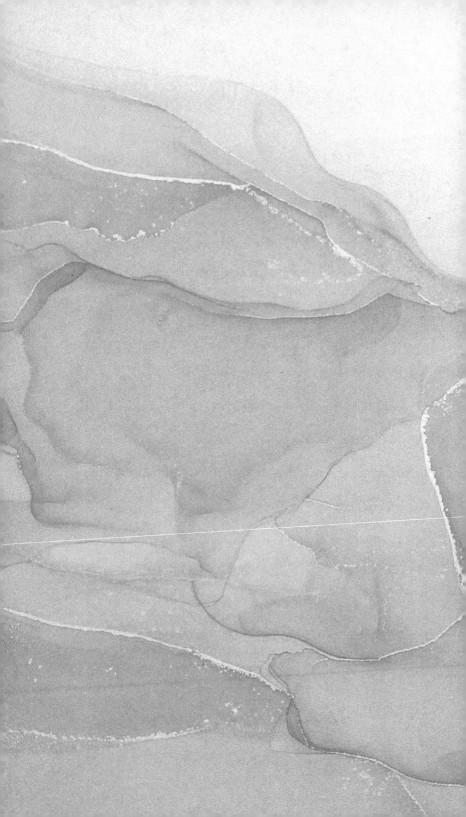

INTRODUCTION

Many of us journey through life pondering the reasons behind our actions and how we can enrich our lives. We seek not only improvement but also a sense of tranquility, productivity, and purpose. Conversations with friends, colleagues, mentors, and partners often echo the advice to "do the work." This phrase never fails to elicit a knowing smile because if it were that simple, we would already be immersed in the process of "doing the work." Yet we continually find ourselves returning to the fundamental question: What is the work?

A deep understanding of oneself is necessary to live a life brimming with abundance, creativity, joy, and love. Self-awareness is a journey inward, a voyage to explore how we present ourselves to the world, and the Enneagram will serve as our guide. Clues about our true selves are sometimes scattered before us, but we often choose to look away from anything that challenges our self-image. This is why the voyage inward, toward self-realization, becomes indispensable in uncovering our genuine, authentic selves.

This journal is thoughtfully crafted to accompany you on this very journey as you harness the insights of the Enneagram. Within these pages you'll encounter an array of writing prompts, mindfulness exercises, inspirational quotes, and grounding meditations for introspection. Each page is a deliberate step along your unique path. It's crucial to remember that this process cannot be hurried or coerced. Guidance on this voyage comes from a source known by many names—God, the Universe, the Divine, Spirit, or a name entirely personal to your experience. All these concepts are interconnected. You need not adhere to any dogmatic religious structure; what truly matters is connecting with that part of you that acknowledges a higher force, shaping and influencing your choices and your path forward.

This journal isn't something you casually dip into; rather, it's an invitation to cultivate a consistent habit of exploring its pages, allowing you to fully embrace the practices within. These pages are designed to guide you toward a profound understanding of why you do what you do.

The Enneagram stands out as a radiant gem among the many personality typing systems, and it beckons with a warm, unique approach centered on uncovering motivations rather than mere behaviors. It opens a doorway to explore the why behind our actions, inviting us to discover the roots of our behaviors. As we delve into this exploration, we find newfound flexibility, unlocking exciting possibilities we may have never imagined before.

We encourage you to delve deeper into the understanding of your dominant Enneagram energy, which is akin to picking up a mirror to gaze upon yourself in a way you've never done before. The idea may initially seem a bit intimidating, but the richness of your life is directly linked to the depth you're willing to explore within your soul.

Your life inherently possesses meaning, purpose, and a trajectory leading toward goodness; it's our natural inclination. Sometimes, we find ourselves needing to reconnect with what truly matters. We might start to wonder and feel disoriented when we sense that we've drifted away from our guiding light. But remember, that guidance hasn't abandoned us; it's possible we've simply strayed from it, unable to see what's right in front of us.

As you embark on this journey, we wish you all the goodness and benefits it has to offer. It's not about reaching a final destination but about following your guiding light, aligning yourself with what's genuine, trustworthy, and good in both the world and within yourself. Return to the pages of this journal daily, allowing your journey to inform you and lead you toward truth, joy, love, light, and goodness. All these elements reside within you, and they'll never abandon you. Sources of love and joy perpetually surround us, and by embracing the truth of goodness in the world, you'll radiate with the light found inside yourself.

This journal is designed as your reference guide and exploratory workbook. The following section will gently guide you through the Enneagram system and provide an overview of Type Seven energy. Within these pages, you'll find a wealth of knowledge about the Enneagram; and using this journal is a chance to reignite your inner connection with your Enneagram Seven energy. Prepare yourself, for your mind will be engaged, your heart will be touched, and your body will respond; all of these experiences, both uplifting and challenging, are an integral part of the journey. We hope you continue to revisit these pages as you further your journey deeper into the Enneagram system.

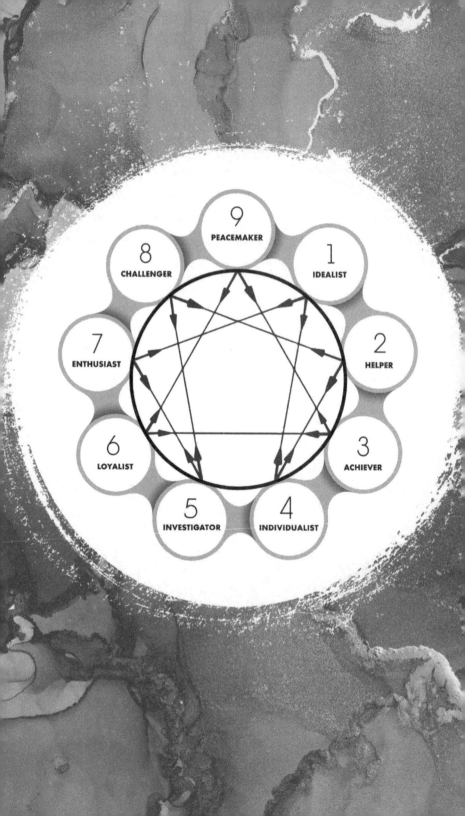

The Enneagram

The Enneagram is an archetypal personality system that combines modern psychological practices with a deep foundation in ancient traditions, religions, cultures, and spiritual practices. It is a model of the human psyche taught as a typology of nine personality archetypes. These types have names that reflect the nine different energies: Eight, Challenger; Nine, Peacemaker; One, Idealist; Two, Helper; Three, Achiever; Four, Individualist; Five, Investigator; Six, Loyalist; and Seven, Enthusiast.

The Enneagram invites you to embark on a journey of self-discovery, unlocking the intricate mechanisms governing your existence. It allows you to delve into the why behind your actions and the how of your daily functioning in pursuit of fulfilling your needs. Unveiling your core motivations, values, fears, and inherent strengths is a perpetual source of insight. Simultaneously, the Enneagram casts light on the egoic patterns that occasionally hinder our progress, thwarting our alignment with our true selves. More significantly, while this insightful system aids us in uncovering our authentic selves, it equally guides us in connecting with others, fostering appreciation, and cultivating genuine presence.

This beginning section is designed to serve as a refresher on the basics of the Enneagram and a quick look into each of the nine types. Remember: the Enneagram is a fluid system that provides access to all nine types, and we encourage you to explore your relationship with all of these energies.

The moment you intentionally chose to use this journal, you began your journey to discover who you really are instead of creating another version of yourself. Or, as people like to say, "the best version of yourself." Your goal now is to find out who you are underneath all the versions of yourself that you have created. Welcome to the journey of your lifetime! May you find joy, peace, acceptance, and belonging in this exploration. May love be your path, and may light shine on every step you take. Most importantly, may you fall deeply in love with the authentic you. The glorious being that you were created to be.

A QUICK OVERVIEW OF THE BASICS OF THE ENNEAGRAM

TYPE/POINT

Each of the nine Enneagram points possesses unique energies and characteristics. When discussing an Enneagram type, we are identifying the specific point on the Enneagram where one embodies the most significant energy. It's important to note that we have access to all nine points on the Enneagram, each contributing to our holistic understanding and personal growth.

CENTERS OF INTELLIGENCE

The Enneagram is explored through three Centers of Intelligence: Body, Heart, and Head. Sometimes, these centers, or triads, are called Body/Instinctive, Heart/Feeling, and Head/Thinking. Each center has a connection to particular emotions: the Body, anger and rage (Eight, Nine, One); the Heart, shame and guilt (Two, Three, Four); and the Head, fear and anxiety (Five, Six, Seven).

BASIC DESIRE AND BASIC FEAR

We all have inner drive and internalized fear that affect all of our behaviors, beliefs, and actions. You may resonate with all nine basic fears and desires, as we are beings composed of all nine energies; however, you will have the most substantial connection to one corresponding fear and desire of one specific type.

CORE MOTIVATION

The core motivation constantly challenges us to get what we most desire at any given moment while avoiding what we fear that will cause our demise. The core motivation is your internal drive, the reason you wake up in the morning, how you navigate life, and that thing that gets you going or paralyzes you. Think of the core motivation as why you do what you do.

WINGS

The types on either side of your dominant Enneagram energy affect how your type shows up in the world. Every Enneagram type has two wings; however, one of the wings may significantly influence the energy of your dominant Enneagram type.

Lines and Arrows

The Enneagram lines and arrows, also referred to as the stress and security points or directions of growth and stress, connect the types across the map. There are multiple ways of using the lines and arrows when we see them as connections to pick up specific qualities at specific times. We can move freely between these connections, picking up positive and negative energies as we need them to create a warning system and a path for growth.

Passion: The Way We Suffer—Personal Challenge

The passions represent the nine main ways we lose our center, become more susceptible to personality distortions, and become disoriented from reality. We can refer to each of the passions as the way in which each type suffers.

Fixation: How We Get Stuck—The Trap

We all have a way of becoming trapped in our personality, which we see play out through the fixation. These "traps" are mental blocks we hold on to when attempting to justify our reality.

Virtue: Our True Nature—The Gift

Honoring our true selves and who we become develops when we land in our virtue. These specific characteristics manifest through the emotional awareness of the authentic self, and the letting go of ego, self-deception, and dynamic vices. When we access our virtue, we become selfless and altruistic in our actions, feelings, and beliefs.

Instincts

The Instincts, sometimes referred to as Subtypes and Instinctual Variants, within each Enneagram energy are Self-Preservation, Social, and Sexual (sometimes referred to as One-on-One). The Instincts can be mirrored in the three drives for survival: preserving life and focusing on physical needs, mutual cooperation and creating social bonds, and species survival through exploration and experiencing energies. We have a dominant instinct that we feel most comfortable with and a secondary instinct to support the dominant one. The third instinct is usually the least developed, therefore, an area that manifests as an unseen personal challenge.

LEVELS OF DEVELOPMENT

The Levels of Development established by Don Riso and Russ Hudson demonstrate the varying degrees of how each type can show up in the world based on presence. Healthy, average, and unhealthy refer to the Levels of Development and the overall state of a person's ability to function. The energy of each type can show up very differently depending on how healthy or unhealthy the individual is; this is a common reason why many people mistype or feel uncomfortable as their dominant type.

Healthy—Becoming expansive and unconstricted in essence, fully present in the world

Average—Beginning to allow our egos to guide our behaviors, dropping into destructive patterns when we fall asleep to our true selves, with a fluctuation of presence

Unhealthy—Dysfunctional and destructive behaviors when ego becomes the driving force behind everything we do; falling into ego-based patterns that trap us in personality

HEALTHY	L1	BEING	Freedom from Ego Structure
	L2	ALLOWING	Psychological Capacity ("I Am")
	L3	DOING	Social Value / Gift
AVERAGE	L4	EFFORTING	Social Role / Imbalance
	L5	IMPOSING	Interpersonal Control
	L6	AGGRESSION	Overcompensation
UNHEALTHY	L7	VIOLATING	Violation
	L8	COMPULSIVE	Delusion & Compulsion
	L9	DESTROYING	Pathological Destruction

ADAPTED FROM THE RISO-HUDSON LEVELS OF DEVELOPMENT

THINGS TO REMEMBER

- There are nine points on the Enneagram map. We can access all the points but lead with one dominant type. The numbers are not a scale, meaning no type is better or worse than any other type. However, in order to keep the Enneagram energies grouped by the centers of intelligence, we look at the types in this order: Eight, Nine, One, Two, Three, Four, Five, Six, Seven.

- Your dominant Enneagram type does not change throughout your life or shift based on your home or work life. You are born into your type and your experiences adjust how you navigate life, access your wing energy, travel with the arrows, and drop into the Levels of Development.

- No type is inherently gendered or dependent on dimensions of diversity (perceived race, socioeconomic status, education, age, religion, etc.). While the descriptions and energies of the types are universal and are not dependent on certain identifying factors, it is essential to note how an Enneagram energy can vary based on cultural or environmental influences or psychological well-being. For instance, some cultures have specific gender roles, socially acceptable values, or religious influences that can impact the Enneagram energy. Still, these factors do not fundamentally change a person's dominant Enneagram type.

- No one can tell you where you stand on the Enneagram map. You find your place by reading about and exploring all aspects of the nine types. Tests can help you narrow down the choices, and you may find your type by process of elimination. Tests are not always the defining factor of where you stand on the Enneagram map; the tests' quality matters.

KEY DESCRIPTORS OF
THE NINE TYPES

The descriptors for each Enneagram type listed below begin on the high side of the energy and transition into the low side of the energy.

THE BODY CENTER

8 self-confident, authoritative, hardworking, strong-willed, forceful, passionate, outspoken, independent, protective, abundant energy, maintaining power and control, defensive, combative, "invulnerable," harsh, rageful, vengeful, boastful, demonstrative, tyrannical, omnipotent

9 receptive, reassuring, agreeable, considerate, quiet, easygoing, thoughtful, accepting, supportive, accommodating, dependable, stable, hardworking, pragmatic, complacent, disengaged, emotionally indolent, indifferent, angry, stubborn, dissociated, numb, apathetic

1 principled, purposeful, organized, ethical, fastidious, fair, objective, sense of mission, practical action, high standards, inner critic, highly critical, impatient, repressed, angry, controlling, perfectionistic, puritanical, resentful, emotionally constricted, scolding, abrasive, punitive, inflexible

THE HEART CENTER

2 generous, empathetic, helpful, thoughtful, caring, reliable, compassionate, kind, overly considerate, people-pleasing, seductive, intrusive, possessive, seeking validation, angry, resentful, hurt, manipulative, flattering, demonstrative, low self-esteem/value

3 hardworking, dedicated, driven, ambitious, resourceful, impressive, motivated, highly skilled, distinguished, pragmatic, opportunistic, calculating, narcissistic, impostor syndrome, seeking validation and attention, social climber, arrogant, unprincipled, self-centered, conceited

4 emotional, empathetic, creative, unique, connected, deep, romantic, authentic, eccentric, poetic, introspective, sensitive, moody, manipulative, judgmental, self-conscious, tormented, dark, depressive, angry, lost, self-destructive, hopeless, despair, macabre, self-absorbed

THE HEAD CENTER

5   competent, capable, cerebral, wise, highly skilled, well-rounded, eccentric, pioneering, complex, perceptive, independent, inventive, visionary, secretive, withdrawn, antagonistic, cynical, argumentative, reclusive, intellectually arrogant, self-destructive, nihilistic, erratic

6   innovative, structured, hardworking, intensely loyal, reliable, security-oriented, troubleshooting, revolutionary, engaging, contradictory, dependent, indecisive, untrusting, defensive, reactive, fearful, insecure, stubborn, suspicious, erratic, worst-case scenario, panicked, paranoid

7   free-spirited, fun, happy, curious, joyful, optimistic, adventurous, fast learners, well-rounded, humorous, bold, vivacious, life of the party, flaky, self-centered, narcissistic, emotionally stunted, insensitive, impulsive, escapist mentality, erratic, compulsive, panic-stricken, avoidance, jaded

Which descriptors from your Enneagram energy
do you resonate with the most and why?

_____

_____

_____

_____

_____

_____

_____

_____

_____

_____

_____

_____

Enneagram Type Seven

DESCRIPTORS FOR SEVEN ENERGY

optimistic, joyful, spontaneous, happy, versatile,
extroverted, multi-talented, playful, curious,
inspirational, high-spirited, excitable, adventurous,
uninhibited, impulsive, scattered, avoidance tendencies,
impatient, hedonistic, detached, judgmental,
insensitive, anxious, self-destructive, jaded

Basic Desire: to be happy, satisfied, and content, to have the freedom of choice, to have needs fulfilled

Basic Fear: to be deprived, to be in pain or experience suffering, to feel trapped, to have freedom compromised

Core Motivation: to maintain your own freedom and happiness, to avoid missing out on worthwhile experiences, to stay excited and occupied, to avoid and deny pain and trauma

Passion/The Personal Challenge: Gluttony—a deep desire to take on more of whatever life has to offer in order to avoid conflict, pain, or feeling trapped

Fixation/The Trap: Planning—a paralyzing pattern of constantly looking for the next best thing, always moving forward, never looking back in search of whatever may bring happiness

Virtue/The Gift: Sobriety—a presence and stillness grounded in authentic internal reflection while accepting the reality of what is and not what could be

Wings: Six and Eight

Arrows: One and Five

Sevens want to be:

- free to seek out more pleasure
- able to keep options open
- able to avoid and discharge pain
- perpetually excited and occupied
- able to maintain freedom and happiness
- free to avoid missing out on anything worthwhile
- open to a wide variety of interesting experiences and choices

Sevens do not want to be:

- trapped or limited by having few choices or options
- bored or in a position to feel guilty
- open to letting anxieties arise for long
- slowed down by others
- still and quiet for long periods of time
- forced to dwell in the past

LEVELS OF DEVELOPMENT AS A TYPE SEVEN

HEALTHY LEVELS OF DEVELOPMENT

As a healthy Seven, you can establish your presence with principled focus and resilience, leading with awareness and profound vision in the face of divisiveness, confrontation, and conflict. You have found stillness and sobriety in the ability to access your authentic self and take right action with laser focus rather than a scattered approach to avoiding pain. The need to find outlets for deflecting pain in the hopes of maintaining a false sense of freedom is transformed into a warning system for you to wake up, slow down, and become present. You no longer bounce from experience to experience, and you are able to acknowledge and find joy in the moment without having to always seek out something new or better. The extraordinary ability to find true happiness and create connections across differences with Grace and optimism is truly astonishing when you step into your true self.

AVERAGE LEVELS OF DEVELOPMENT

Most humans reside within these average levels and fluctuate up or down depending on the circumstances they find themselves in. As you drop down into the average Levels of Development, the ego agenda begins to take over. The fluctuations can create opportunities for you to pause and cultivate the presence needed to examine your thoughts and actions and course correct. This allows you to move back up in the levels and avoid falling back into unhealthy patterns of behavior and thought. However, as the ability for self-reflection and course correction wanes, you can become scattered and tactless, reticent to engage authentically in real emotional honesty for more than a fleeting moment. When challenges arise you tend to be disengaged and dismissive. You become emotionally stunted; in deflecting your authentic self you are now self-seeking and uncomfortable with engaging or remaining present in any space that has conflict, and your apathy toward others is caused by the anxiety of feeling trapped. You can become passive at the sheer volume of suffering in the world and feel helpless and hopeless. You may find short-lived presence and experience a calming sensation when you are able to channel healthy habits. You are able to find a clear focus on how to engage in life, but the fear of getting trapped and not being able to escape the monotony or the fear of jeopardizing your freedom quickly shifts you back into your deflection and evasion tactics. The fear and anxiety at these levels can morph into a combination of deflection, avoidance, and self-centered behaviors and cause you to drop further down the levels. It takes a great deal of self-reflection and inner work to rise through the levels and avoid dropping further.

UNHEALTHY LEVELS OF DEVELOPMENT

As you drop into the unhealthy levels, you become extremely narcissistic, unstable, insensitive, cynical, vindictive, and delusional. You begin to justify your actions and beliefs from the unhealthy energy of Seven. You often inadvertently become trapped in your self-inflicted unhappiness and pain, and feeling helpless you react impulsively and erratically to avoid any real emotional honesty. Fear, denial, and the repression of unhealed wounds are the primary motivators that distort your reality, resulting in a disdain for anything that feels like a challenge to your happiness or freedom. This disconnect may trigger your deep fear of becoming present to yourself, leading to an irresponsible pattern of acting out in panic and heedlessness. As you drop lower into the unhealthy levels, you are only covering up and defending against unhealed wounds that you refuse to truly acknowledge.

You can refer back to the Levels of Development to see where you are at any point in time. Make notes on your progress below:

_____

_____

_____

_____

_____

_____

_____

_____

WINGS

Remember, you have access to both wings. Some people identify strongly with one wing energy over the other, but both wings still affect how your dominant type appears.

Seven with a Strong Six Wing

Sensitive to others' feelings, optimistic in difficult situations, productive and cooperative, anxiety and self-doubt, boredom and a scattered focus, disconnected from emotional honesty

Seven with a Strong Eight Wing

Self-confident and assertive, calm during difficult situations, positive and uplifting for others, naturally charismatic, impatient, harsh, cold, blunt, self-centered and scattered when forced to deal with others

ARROWS

Remember, you have access to both arrows, and you can move freely between these connections. This movement allows you to pick up positive and negative energies as needed and creates a warning system and a path for growth.

Seven's Arrow to One

Principled and grounded, more focused on others and aware of the impact of actions and behaviors, self-centered and judgmental, overly confident and dismissive of others and their feelings

Seven's Arrow to Five

Find calming stillness in self-reflection, thoughtful and kind, satiated and focused, avoid accountability, self-centered and detached from others, narcissistic beliefs

INSTINCTS

As balanced human beings, we naturally have all three instincts within us. However, we have a dominant instinct that we feel most comfortable with and a secondary instinct to support the dominant one. The third instinct is usually the least developed, therefore, an area that manifests as an unseen personal challenge.

SELF-PRESERVATION SEVEN

As a Self-Preservation Seven, you tend to be highly ambitious and work hard to make sure you maintain enough freedom—financial, professional, or personal—to be able to do as you please. You may focus your energy on cultivating a life where you can maximize your experiences and fulfill your desires without having to rely too heavily on anyone or anything. You can be socially motivated, as Sevens tend to be more extroverted than not, but you unknowingly hold on to a deep anxiety around becoming too attached to anyone for fear of feeling trapped or bogged down.

SOCIAL SEVEN

As a Social Seven, you have probably spent considerable time cultivating a group of friends who share similar interests and are ready to take on any adventure. You may enjoy getting involved in social causes, groups, or community activities but your natural tendency to allow your fear of feeling trapped or deprived of freedom makes you feel anxious as you get too comfortable with a single activity or group. You can easily withdraw and revert to evasive behaviors by abandoning people or groups when you feel overwhelmed by responsibility or obligation.

SEXUAL SEVEN

As a Sexual Seven, you may focus your energy on finding new experiences and adventures, you seek out uniqueness and reject the ordinary. You thrive on feeling alive and taking in all that life has to offer. The downside to this energy is the predisposition to get bored easily and to allow your perpetual forward movement to prevent you from sticking with any one person, group, or situation for too long. You may tend to romanticize relationships, enjoying the beginning stages of them, but getting bored easily you may leave a wake of unfulfilled commitments and jilted relationships as you bounce to something new.

SEVEN'S RESPONSES TO CONFLICTS

UNHEALTHY REACTION

Avoidance tendencies, using inappropriate humor, insensitivity, cutting people out of your life, complete denial, anger, overwhelmed exhaustion, feeling trapped causing irrational outbursts, cynicism, "fight-or-flight," insensitivity, self-centered stance, erratic mood swings, callous deflection of others humanity, when triggered you may use your unhealthy energy to dismiss, demean, and dehumanize anyone or anything that forces you to brush up against the darkness lurking inside of you, you may make jokes and point out the pain of others as a way to deflect the responsibility you have to access true compassion as a decent human being

HEALTHY REACTION

Pausing for presence, using charisma to enable others, trailblazing visionary, positivity, inability to watch others suffering forces you into action to spread joy and happiness, general ability to stay positive during tough times, connecting people across differences using your innate power to find the good in any situation, infectious positive energy and natural tenacity to advocate for the acknowledgment of others' pain and suffering and serve as a bridge builder for people from all different backgrounds, grounded presence allows you to stay accountable and focus on what is important

Reflections on your experience of unhealthy and healthy responses:

_____

_____

_____

_____

_____

_____

EXAMPLES OF SEVEN ENERGY

The Dalai Lama, James Baldwin, Suze Orman, John F. Kennedy, Eddie Murphy, Elton John, Robin Williams, Jim Carrey, Ram Dass, Leonardo DiCaprio, Howard Stern, Jeff Bezos, Joe Biden, Sarah Palin, George W. Bush, Betty White, Edward VIII (Duke of Windsor), Thomas Jefferson, Benjamin Franklin, Amelia Earhart, Malcolm Forbes, Richard Branson, Ted Turner

Explore your connection to one or more of these people who demonstrate strong Seven energy. What is it about their character or personality that reminds you most of yourself?

_____

_____

_____

_____

_____

_____

_____

_____

_____

_____

_____

_____

_____

_____

_____

_____

_____

_____

How do you experience the different elements
of Seven energy within yourself?

_____

_____

_____

_____

_____

_____

_____

_____

_____

_____

_____

_____

_____

_____

_____

_____

_____

_____

_____

_____

_____

_____

What is your experience like with other
people who exhibit Seven energy?

_____

_____

_____

_____

_____

_____

_____

_____

_____

_____

_____

_____

_____

_____

_____

_____

_____

_____

_____

_____

_____

Reflections on
BEING AN
ENNEAGRAM SEVEN

As you embark on this inner journey, it's essential to take a moment to revisit the very origin of your path. Within this section, we invite you to reflect upon the beginnings of your Enneagram journey and how it gently unfolded before you. Delving into past feelings and behaviors is a natural and important aspect of this process.

As a Seven, your remarkable strengths lie in your abundance of optimism and charismatic energy. The prompts provided here offer you a special opportunity for profound introspection.

It's quite likely that you had specific reactions when you first discovered your dominant energy as a Type Seven. These reactions are all part of the ongoing journey as you gradually transition from mere reactions to intentional responses. It's essential to explore your feelings but not to become ensnared or overwhelmed by what you feel. Remember, feelings are transient by nature. As you navigate through your emotions, you'll discover immense fulfillment at the deeper layers of this exploration. Embrace your innate curiosity and approach this journey with the wonder of a beginner's mind as you unveil more and more about your authentic self and how you present yourself to the world. In connecting with the reality of your inner guidance and greatness, you may be pleasantly surprised by the fears that once held you back.

It's important to note that not every attribute, characteristic, or behavior described at Type Seven will necessarily resonate with your unique energy experience. This is an incredible opportunity to unearth aspects of your being that have, until now, remained hidden from your conscious awareness. This profound self-discovery journey will open your mind, mend your heart, and rejuvenate your body in ways you may have never imagined. As you dive deep into this exploration, your spirit will gracefully embrace and embody your core values, aligning with your precious gifts of joyfulness and freedom. Don't restrain yourself. Allow your spirit to ascend to levels within your own being that you've never before touched. This is our heartfelt wish for you.

Grounding Meditation

As I move into self-reflection and internal exploration,
I will meditate on these prompts and gently notice
what comes up as I breathe into stillness.

I am ready to begin with three cleansing breaths.

I am releasing any tension that I am holding
in my body with each exhale.

I am grounded and present to the sensations in my body.

I am open and aware of the feelings in my heart.

I am not attached to the thoughts that float by.

I am ready to explore what being a Seven means to me.

I will embrace all aspects of my personality and gently
work toward becoming more accepting of myself.

My reactions when I discovered my dominant energy as a Type Seven:

_____

_____

_____

_____

_____

_____

_____

_____

_____

_____

_____

_____

_____

_____

_____

_____

_____

_____

_____

_____

_____

_____

My feelings about being a Seven:

_____
_____
_____
_____
_____
_____
_____
_____
_____
_____
_____
_____
_____
_____
_____
_____
_____
_____
_____
_____
_____
_____
_____
_____
_____

My hopes for discovering more about my Seven energy:

My fears around seeing myself as I truly am:

_____

_____

_____

_____

_____

_____

_____

_____

_____

_____

_____

_____

_____

_____

_____

_____

_____

_____

_____

_____

_____

Observations about myself that support Seven as my dominant type:

Aspects and descriptors of Seven energy that I do not feel connected to:

_____

_____

_____

_____

_____

_____

_____

_____

_____

_____

Are these aspects I do not feel connected with indicators
of any personal challenges that I may overlook?

_____

_____

_____

_____

_____

_____

_____

_____

What are my core values that align with my Seven energy?

_____

_____

_____

_____

_____

_____

_____

_____

_____

_____

_____

_____

_____

_____

_____

_____

_____

_____

_____

Reflections on my actions and beliefs around my core values:

Ways I have honored my core values recently:

_____

_____

_____

_____

_____

_____

_____

_____

_____

_____

_____

_____

_____

_____

_____

_____

_____

_____

_____

_____

_____

_____

_____

_____

What do I wish people knew about me?

_____
_____
_____
_____
_____
_____
_____
_____
_____
_____
_____
_____
_____
_____
_____
_____
_____
_____
_____
_____
_____
_____
_____
_____

Reflections on

MY EARLY MESSAGES AND EXPERIENCES

As you embark on this journey, take a moment to reflect on the early messages and messengers that have shaped your path. You might discover that your childhood experiences with the powerful energy of Type Seven instilled in you a strong desire for freedom.

These initial reactions and responses, etched deep within you, were not merely fleeting notions but lasting imprints. You absorbed messages you may not have been consciously aware of, and they didn't simply pass through; instead, they were deeply ingrained in your very being. Retrieving them intentionally requires the assistance of a profound inner exploration. As you transitioned into adulthood, these feelings became an integral part of your approach to life. You might have developed an internal narrative that guides you to gaze ahead, to map your course toward the future, and to explore fresh opportunities that would safeguard your precious freedom. This inner narrative, a soothing balm for your soul, served to quell the waves of anxiety and prevent the haunting specter of deprivation or confinement from casting its shadow. In its own unique way, it became an integral part of your journey, a compass for your choices, but it also may have led you to develop some challenging patterns of behavior.

In looking back, you may begin to discern specific ways in which you aligned with the energy of Seven. As you reflect on your life's unfolding, who or what stands out as a pivotal influence in your development? Comparing and contrasting your life experiences, the individuals who left lasting imprints, and the indelible impressions etched in your heart is an integral part of this introspective expedition.

As a Type Seven, you may have cultivated a natural inclination to tiptoe around anything from your past that may have cast a fleeting shadow of negativity. But we invite you to do something extraordinary—embrace it, explore it, for what remains buried can never truly be addressed.

The journey from Seven to the more grounded energies of the Enneagram might seem like a daunting path, but it holds the key to genuine joy, serenity, gratitude, and love. Delve deeper into the realms of your childhood, both its bright moments and its fleeting shadows. Recall the treasures of joy that once sparkled in your life as a child. Let those memories be the guiding stars that lead you to rediscover the immense wellspring of joy and gratitude waiting for you in this season of your life. It's a journey that promises to unveil the most radiant facets of your authentic self.

Grounding Meditation

As I move into self-reflection and internal exploration,
I will meditate on these prompts and gently notice
what comes up as I breathe into stillness.

I am ready to begin with three cleansing breaths.

I am inhaling peace and exhaling tension.

I am ready to embark on a journey into my past.

I will honor my experience as I recall childhood memories.

My past does not define me.

I can explore what was, accept what is, and embrace what will be.

My most vivid memory of how my Seven energy
showed up when I was a child:

_____

_____

_____

_____

_____

_____

_____

_____

_____

_____

_____

_____

_____

_____

_____

_____

_____

_____

_____

_____

People and experiences that have brought me
the most joy and meaning in life:

_____

_____

_____

_____

_____

_____

_____

_____

_____

_____

_____

_____

_____

_____

_____

_____

_____

_____

_____

_____

_____

I can create space in my life for more of these positive influences by:

_____

_____

_____

_____

_____

_____

_____

_____

_____

_____

_____

_____

_____

_____

_____

_____

_____

_____

_____

_____

_____

_____

What are some memories I tend to reframe into positives when
I should be looking at the reality of what I experienced?

_____

_____

_____

_____

_____

_____

_____

_____

_____

_____

_____

_____

_____

_____

_____

_____

_____

_____

_____

_____

_____

_____

Activities I enjoyed as a child:

_____

_____

_____

_____

_____

_____

_____

_____

_____

_____

_____

_____

_____

_____

_____

_____

_____

_____

_____

_____

_____

Reflections on how these activities
brought feelings of pure joy and happiness:

_____

_____

_____

_____

_____

_____

_____

_____

_____

_____

_____

_____

_____

_____

_____

_____

_____

_____

_____

_____

_____

_____

_____

Happiness is part
of the flow of life.

If you remain rigid,
then happiness will
flow right past you.

Allow yourself
the gift of letting
go and ease into the
flow of whatever may
come your way.

I can cultivate small moments of happiness in my everyday life by:

Reflections on

MY PURPOSE AND MY "PUZZLE PIECE"

Let's imagine the world as a puzzle, and envision each one of us holding a piece that, when placed, helps create a more complete and harmonious world. You possess a truly unique gift to offer to the world; imagine it as if you are the holder of a vital piece of a grand, intricate puzzle. Yet to truly offer this gift, we must be willing to embark on our own inner journey.

When we embrace this inner work, we gain the strength and clarity needed to step forward and make our unique contribution. This courageous act sets a beautiful chain reaction in motion, allowing others to find the inspiration and courage to contribute as well.

In the upcoming section, we extend a warm invitation to you, encouraging you to (re)awaken the passions and interests that stir deep within your soul, those beautiful aspects of yourself that you'd love to revive and share with the world. You might notice a strong emotional response to social injustices; this very reaction could be a hidden passion or a point of personal growth waiting to be unveiled. Your dedication to a particular societal issue could hold the key to discovering your unique place and voice in contributing to the collective healing of humanity. Perhaps your heart resonates deeply with environmental causes, or you're deeply affected by the suffering of animals. This is your precious opportunity to unearth and delve into what truly matters to you.

Consider what consistently draws your attention and captivates your mind—whether it's art, music, literature, social causes, theater, science, spirituality, parenting, or family. Why do these topics continue to surface for you? Use this opportunity to delve deeper into the aspects of your life where you find an abundance of energy or even areas that may initially appear exhausting. This is your chance to sculpt and refine your unique puzzle piece (and yes, we all have one or more) so that you can stand with gratitude and presence, fully aware of the significance of your contribution. As we awaken to our own purpose, we naturally have the capacity to awaken those around us, igniting a chain reaction of positive change.

Explore the boundless possibilities that lie ahead, and remember that your piece of the puzzle is invaluable to creating a world that's more complete, compassionate, and connected.

Grounding Meditation

As I move into self-reflection and internal exploration,
I will meditate on these prompts and gently notice
what comes up as I breathe into stillness.

I am ready to begin with three cleansing breaths.

I am releasing any tension that I am holding
in my body with each exhale.

I am inhaling into the wholeness of the Universe
and exhaling whatever may be troubling me.

I am open to exploring my place in the world.

I am willing to explore my purpose and (re)discover the
unique puzzle piece I hold to contribute to the world.

My life has meaning, and my presence matters.

I am accepting of whatever comes up for me at this moment.

What contributions do I want to make in this world?

Reflections on how I align my daily actions with my deeper
sense of finding joy and seeking out pleasure:

_____

_____

_____

_____

_____

_____

_____

_____

_____

_____

_____

_____

_____

_____

_____

_____

_____

_____

_____

_____

_____

What inspires me?

How have I limited myself in finding sources of inspiration? How can I open myself to new experiences? Have I considered engaging with new people, places, music, art, literature, and so on?

I am very passionate about:

_____

_____

_____

_____

_____

_____

_____

_____

_____

_____

_____

_____

_____

_____

_____

_____

_____

_____

_____

_____

_____

What comes up for me when I think about the activities, relationships, and causes that I am drawn to?

The quality of your life will reflect how deep you are willing to go to touch your own soul.

What personal, professional, spiritual, and/or life
roles contribute to my sense of identity?

_____
_____
_____
_____
_____
_____
_____
_____
_____
_____
_____
_____
_____
_____
_____
_____
_____
_____
_____
_____

What does it look like when I become bored or disinterested in things I used to be passionate about?

How can I use my natural charisma and abundance of energy
to inspire others, and what does that look like?

_____

_____

_____

_____

_____

_____

_____

_____

_____

_____

_____

_____

_____

_____

_____

_____

_____

_____

_____

_____

Reflections on my current projects, work, and/or endeavors:

How are these feeding my spirit or draining my energy?

HOW MY SEVEN ENERGY SHOWS UP

As a Seven, your inner compass is guided by a profound and beautiful value—freedom. This value infuses every facet of your existence, casting a colorful tapestry of experiences and shaping the way your unique energy unfolds in the world. When your happiness and freedom remain untarnished, you stand tall, feeling justified in your actions, comfortable in your own skin, yet still yearning for more, ever so eager to explore what the world has to offer.

You possess a strong need to safeguard your options as Seven, a desire that springs to life in situations marked by a multitude of priorities, obligations, and a sprinkle of risk. It's here that the blueprint for your standards takes shape and the symphony of your life begins to play its tune.

Yet there are moments when the grounded stance you've cultivated slips away, giving way to the allure of instant pleasure over steadfast trustworthiness. This is when the desire to enhance your life takes a different turn, leading to a hedonistic "me-first" mentality that can sometimes cloud your vision. It's at this juncture that the call for inner work becomes clear—a journey to raise the vibrational frequency of your energy and realign your ceaseless quest for "more" with a balanced perspective.

As you embark on this profound inner journey, you gradually shed the weight of judgment and the relentless, and sometimes aimless, pursuit of happiness. Instead, you open the door to a realm where deep joy, love, freedom, and a genuine commitment to your relationships and responsibilities guide your steps. No longer bound by the quest for external thrills and excitement, you begin to discover the profound joy nestled within your present circumstances and the richness of your connections with others. There's no incessant longing for a better tomorrow, for you've learned to relish the gift of life in each passing moment.

In this daily state of presence, your very being becomes a welcoming beacon. You're received with open hearts and open minds, your influence on the world around you cherished and valued. The joy and light you radiate touches the lives of those fortunate enough to cross your path, a profound testament to the transformative power of embracing the flow of life as the precious gift that it is. In this space of profound presence and joy, your journey continues to unfold, and the world rejoices with you.

Grounding Meditation

As I move into self-reflection and internal exploration,
I will meditate on these prompts and gently notice
what comes up as I breathe into stillness.

I am ready to begin with three cleansing breaths.

I am releasing any tension that I am holding
in my body with each exhale.

I am inhaling into presence and exhaling anxiety.

I am ready to explore my Sevenness.

I will allow myself to reflect on how I show up to myself and others.

I will acknowledge any anxiety and worry that arises
with Grace and compassion for myself.

I will embrace all parts of my being as valid and valuable.

I will release the need to avoid the tough stuff and
allow myself to honor whatever may surface.

Reflect back on the "Levels of Development" section (page 14) for this exercise.

I was aware of the high side of my Seven energy this week when:

_____

_____

_____

_____

_____

_____

_____

_____

_____

_____

_____

_____

_____

_____

_____

_____

_____

_____

_____

_____

Reflect back on the "Levels of Development" section (page 14) for this exercise.

I was aware of the low side of my Seven energy this week when:

_____

_____

_____

_____

_____

_____

_____

_____

_____

_____

_____

_____

_____

_____

_____

_____

_____

_____

_____

_____

_____

_____

_____

Joy calls out to us
to recognize and savor
the daily moments
in our life experiences
that ignite our spirits
and enrich our lives.
These moments help
us surrender to the
involuntary smile
that often comes from
unexpected sources.

My reflections on finding joy and what it means to me:

_____

_____

_____

_____

_____

_____

_____

_____

_____

_____

_____

_____

_____

_____

_____

_____

_____

_____

_____

_____

_____

_____

_____

My reactions to feeling trapped:

_____
_____
_____
_____
_____
_____
_____
_____
_____
_____
_____
_____
_____
_____
_____
_____
_____
_____
_____
_____
_____
_____
_____
_____

Ways that I experience challenges to my freedom:

_____

_____

_____

_____

_____

_____

_____

_____

_____

_____

_____

_____

_____

_____

_____

_____

_____

_____

_____

_____

_____

_____

_____

_____

_____

What parts of myself do I hide from others and why?

_____

_____

_____

_____

_____

_____

_____

_____

_____

_____

_____

_____

_____

_____

_____

_____

_____

_____

_____

_____

_____

How do I express love and affection?

When do I feel understood and appreciated?

_____

_____

_____

_____

_____

_____

_____

_____

_____

_____

_____

_____

_____

_____

_____

_____

_____

_____

_____

_____

_____

_____

What does it look like when someone doesn't understand me?

You must embrace your own being and accept yourself exactly as you are. This is a first step in belonging. Never let anyone determine whether or not you belong.

That choice is yours.

What does belonging mean to me? How have I sought
out belonging and connection in my life?

_____

_____

_____

_____

_____

_____

_____

_____

_____

_____

_____

_____

_____

_____

_____

_____

_____

_____

_____

_____

_____

What do other people do for me that makes me feel seen?

How do I make others feel seen?

How do other people describe me?

Fill the page with words, phrases, and drawings.
Allow for the flow of creativity and freedom.

How do I describe myself?

Fill the page with words, phrases, and drawings.
Allow for the flow of creativity and freedom.

Reflections on
EMOTIONS AND
AVOIDANCE TENDENCIES

As a Seven, you've embarked on a journey where the vibrant energy of your personality often intersects with the challenge of embracing and navigating your emotions. Your Seven energy, like a fluttering butterfly, tends to shy away from pain and discomfort. It gracefully, and sometimes ungracefully, flutters over certain emotions to safeguard its precious reserves of joy, optimism, and freedom.

In your quest to uphold these cherished qualities, you might have, at times, encountered a recurring theme—being perceived as someone who lacks compassion, sensitivity, or consideration. The very aversion to suffering that propels you to sidestep certain emotions may, on occasion, paint you as cold or heartless in the eyes of others. This disconnect, though it may seem daunting, can be thoughtfully addressed and lovingly reestablished through the practices of presence and stillness.

It is important to recognize that even if your intentions are good, you may not always fully grasp the actual impact of your words and behaviors. When your instinct is to distance yourself from discomfort or conflict, you may inadvertently place yourself in a space where, as you descend within the Levels of Development, you begin to exhibit traits such as narcissism, emotional instability, insensitivity, cynicism, and detachment. In these moments, you may find yourself justifying your actions and beliefs from the less healthy energy of Seven, feeling ensnared in your self-inflicted unhappiness and pain. Sometimes this can lead to feelings of helplessness and can trigger impulsive and erratic reactions as a defense mechanism to avoid the genuine emotional honesty that lies beneath the surface.

In this section you are invited to embark on an exploration into your emotions and certain patterns of behavior, not as a harsh judge, but as a patient and understanding observer. Know that you are never trapped in any challenges that may come your way, and you are free to navigate them with the intentional presence that you cultivate. Reflect on the prompts provided, and in this intentional safe space nurture the stillness within you, which will be your guiding light in navigating whatever emotions surface. This is an opportunity to embrace your emotional landscape with a warm and open heart.

Grounding Meditation

As I move into self-reflection and internal exploration,
I will meditate on these prompts and gently notice
what comes up as I breathe into stillness.

I am ready to begin with three cleansing breaths.

I am inhaling into presence and positivity and
exhaling cynicism and negativity.

I acknowledge and accept all of my emotions as part of who I am.

My emotions fluctuate, and I will not get trapped
in discomfort by dealing with them.

I will access Grace and presence as I honor
the function of my emotions.

I will remain in presence and choose a path of
empathy and compassion for myself.

I will begin to take responsibility for how I handle emotions
and resist the urge to sidestep real emotional honesty.

How do my emotions fluctuate?

_____

_____

_____

_____

_____

_____

_____

_____

_____

_____

_____

_____

_____

_____

_____

_____

_____

_____

_____

_____

_____

_____

What emotions do I tend to avoid? Can I explore
this deeper and find out why?

_____

_____

_____

_____

_____

_____

_____

_____

_____

_____

_____

_____

_____

_____

_____

_____

_____

_____

_____

_____

As I bring to mind a strong memory from my life, can I recall what emotions arose and what my process was for dealing with them? Can I do this with two or three strong memories? Consider memories that were good, bad, happy, sad, exciting, disappointing, and so on.

_____

_____

_____

_____

_____

_____

_____

_____

_____

_____

_____

_____

_____

_____

_____

_____

_____

_____

_____

_____

What steps can I take to pause and change my course of action when I notice myself stepping away from real emotional honesty?

_____

_____

_____

_____

_____

_____

_____

_____

_____

_____

_____

_____

_____

_____

_____

_____

_____

_____

_____

_____

What does it look like when I lean in versus step away
to/from emotionally charged situations?

_____

_____

_____

_____

_____

_____

_____

_____

_____

_____

_____

_____

_____

_____

_____

_____

_____

_____

_____

_____

_____

Reflecting back on how I may have been insensitive to other people's expressed feelings and emotions, how could I have handled certain situations differently?

What makes me uncomfortable, and how do I deal with those feelings?

When have I dealt with a particularly painful
situation, and how did I feel afterward?

_____

_____

_____

_____

_____

_____

_____

_____

_____

_____

_____

_____

_____

_____

_____

_____

_____

_____

_____

_____

_____

_____

_____

What am I missing out on when I remove myself from situations that challenge my freedom and avoid emotional honesty? Can I explore a few real-life examples that have happened in the past?

_____

_____

_____

_____

_____

_____

_____

_____

_____

_____

_____

_____

_____

_____

_____

_____

_____

_____

_____

_____

_____

_____

What am I willing to let go of in order to allow myself to begin to deal with emotions and remain present when faced with challenges?

_____

_____

_____

_____

_____

_____

_____

_____

_____

_____

_____

_____

_____

_____

_____

_____

_____

_____

_____

_____

_____

We are surrounded
by Grace in every
moment of our lives.
Grace always comes
through when we allow
ourselves to embrace
and experience the
warmth of its existence.
Let love and light in.

Allow Grace to
lead your actions today.

What does Grace look like for me as a Seven?

MY RELATIONSHIP TO ANXIETY AND FEAR

As a Seven, you might encounter a formidable wall of fear and anxiety, one that may guard an unhealed or unexplored internal wound. This wall can act as a barrier, preventing you from accessing your authentic self, and how you address or ignore it can vary from person to person. For some, this fear might originate from early memories of feeling insecure, unsafe, overwhelmed, unsupported, unfulfilled, or alone. Each individual copes with their fear uniquely, but when we find ourselves trapped in unhealthy patterns of behavior and belief, this internal fear can often manifest outwardly, aimed at deflecting our own fears onto others in some way or another.

Like all of us, your quest for happiness is a universal longing. However, your pursuit of joy and contentment has taken on a unique hue—it's a lifelong adventure designed to keep you afloat, steering clear of the depths of pain you may have encountered. You radiate an unmistakable energy, a vibrant and joyful spirit, and your zest for adventure and excitement is palpable. You savor every flavor that life has to offer, indulging in the rich buffet of experiences.

Beneath this ceaseless movement and exuberance, there often resides a deeply buried sense of dread and pain. There lies a fear that acknowledging what's underneath your buoyant exterior might trap you or lead to feelings of deprivation and discomfort. The reasons behind this perpetual motion and your active resistance against anything that might potentially bind you vary, but one common thread is the avoidance of dealing with genuine emotions or a challenging internal narrative.

In this section, you're given the opportunity to reflect and explore the landscape of your anxiety and fear, and to approach these emotions in a productive and nurturing manner. It's important to stay present, to honor what surfaces within you. As a Seven, resist the urge to sidestep emotional honesty, and hold fast to your presence with a spirit of perseverance and understanding. Be patient with yourself and embrace self-compassion as you venture deeper into this exploration. These exercises are thoughtfully designed to guide you through the depths of your energy's challenges, enabling you to reconnect with the radiant reservoir of goodness, love, and light that resides within you. It's another step toward self-discovery and deeper connection to your authentic self.

Grounding Meditation

As I move into self-reflection and internal exploration,
I will meditate on these prompts and gently notice
what comes up as I breathe into stillness.

I am ready to begin with three cleansing breaths.

I am inhaling a sense of calm and peace and
exhaling tension and anxiety.

I acknowledge my fear and anxiety, and I am willing
to gently explore what's underneath.

I will explore my relationship to my fear
with perseverance and stillness.

I will explore my relationship to my anxiety with
intentional patience and understanding.

I accept fear and anxiety as natural human emotions.

My fear does not define who I am.

My anxiety cannot control me.

I will accept my fear and anxiety as an internal warning system
to seek out opportunities for growth and self-reflection.

What/who makes me anxious or fearful?

What is the difference between these two emotions,
and what does it look like for me personally?

_____

_____

_____

_____

_____

_____

_____

_____

_____

_____

_____

_____

_____

_____

_____

_____

_____

_____

_____

_____

_____

_____

How do I express my anxiety and fear? What does it look like?

I notice I redirect my anxiety by:

_____
_____
_____
_____
_____
_____
_____
_____
_____
_____
_____
_____
_____
_____
_____
_____
_____
_____
_____
_____
_____
_____
_____

What does getting trapped in pain and suffering look like for me?
How does it make me feel to consider this question?

What makes me feel fulfilled and content?

_____

_____

_____

_____

_____

_____

_____

_____

_____

_____

_____

_____

_____

_____

_____

_____

_____

_____

_____

_____

_____

_____

_____

What does it look like when my anxiety takes over?

How have I handled my anxiety in the past? What steps
did I take to properly process my anxiety?

_____

_____

_____

_____

_____

_____

_____

_____

_____

_____

_____

_____

_____

_____

_____

_____

_____

_____

_____

_____

What are some ways I can use my anxiety as an internal warning system to pause and find the grounded presence I need to deal with what is in front of me? Can I come up with specific examples and test them out?

What stresses me out, and what are my reactions?

_____

_____

_____

_____

_____

_____

_____

_____

_____

What are a few small things I can do to relieve my stress?

_____

_____

_____

_____

_____

_____

_____

_____

_____

_____

_____

_____

Reflections on
MY VIRTUE OF
SOBRIETY

A grounding virtue gently awaits you as a Type Seven—sobriety. It's an inviting concept, one that can be embraced as the serene stillness of your presence, a space that invites the abundance of life to flow in, open and adorned with gratitude. Sobriety's gift is the ability to find contentment and joy in the present, with a crystal-clear focus and a profoundly powerful energy that is grounded yet abundant. Sobriety takes its form when you wholeheartedly commit to the inner work and access the gifts residing on the high side of Seven.

Along the path toward your virtue, you might encounter familiar roadblocks. The fixation of planning as a Seven can be a particularly challenging hurdle. It's born from a fear of being ensnared in pain and suffering, a fear that propels you to keep moving forward, seeking outlets that make you feel alive, free, and happy, all while allowing you to sidestep whatever may be lurking in the shadows. This is where the transformative inner work process comes into play.

As you work through these roadblocks, you gradually gain confidence in your ability to be still and relish the joy and opportunities that unfurl before you in the present. The fear of feeling trapped or deprived of your freedom starts to recede. In cultivating stillness and sobriety, you open the door to accessing your authentic self. Taking the right action with laser focus becomes second nature, and you no longer scatter your energies in a quest to avoid pain. Your longing for outlets to deflect the negative morphs into a gentle warning system—a call to wake up and be present. No longer are you confined to a life of bouncing from experience to experience. You discover the profound joy that exists in the moment without a constant craving for something new or better.

Through the embrace of sobriety and the nurturing of stillness, you establish the balance and focus that lead you back to true happiness and connection. Your invitation to delve into this transformative space is an opportunity to reclaim your presence and stillness, transforming you into an openly receptive vessel for connection, joy, and happiness. This is where you can gracefully step into your virtue of sobriety, finding your equilibrium and unwavering focus. Exploring the path to this virtue is yet another step on your journey of unearthing your authentic self, where the embrace of acceptance, gratitude, and true joy awaits.

Grounding Meditation

As I move into self-reflection and internal exploration,
I will meditate on each of these prompts and gently notice
what comes up for me as I breathe into stillness.

I am ready to begin with three cleansing breaths.

I am releasing any tension that I am holding
in my body with each exhale.

I am allowing myself the gift of peace and
stillness as I begin this exploration.

As I explore sobriety, I seek out opportunities
to allow it to flow naturally.

Sobriety is my access to Grace.

Sobriety is always present within me.

I allow myself to embrace the gift of sobriety by
releasing what no longer serves me.

How has sobriety manifested in my life, and what did it bring?

How has sobriety eluded me?
What comes up for me by asking this question?

What am I willing to surrender to embrace sobriety?

When do I notice my tendency toward planning beginning to fade
and my ability to access the virtue of sobriety developing?

_____

_____

_____

_____

_____

_____

_____

_____

_____

_____

_____

_____

_____

_____

_____

_____

_____

_____

Sobriety is the soul's embrace of our true self with unwavering faith that all we seek is already here.

Reflecting on my relationship to anxiety and my avoidance tendencies,
can I explore what my path to the embodiment of sobriety looks like?

What are a few small actions I can take right now to bring myself into the present moment, such as taking a deep breath, stretching, going for a run, or savoring a sip of tea or coffee?

What are a few mantras I will use daily to bring myself back to the present and move into a space where I can access the virtue of sobriety?

*Example: I will stay present in the moment and
find gratitude for whatever life has to offer me.*

Discovering Connections to
OTHER ENNEAGRAM ENERGIES

Consider the Enneagram energies as nine individual gifts, each uniquely enriching the tapestry of your being. Within each of us, these nine energies coexist, and far too often, our fixation on our Enneagram type limits our perspective, hindering exploration of the eight other invaluable energies residing within us. It's vital to recognize that every human being requires the presence of these nine energies to achieve wholeness and completeness.

At each point of the Enneagram, a precious gift awaits, illuminating the path of self-discovery. At point One the gift is integrity, a beacon that guides you with a resolute moral compass. Point Two bestows the gift of pure love, fostering a spirit of generosity and an open heart for giving and receiving. Point Three endows you with the drive to accomplish and achieve great things, not just for personal gain but for the greater good of all. Point Four graces you with the capacity to embrace the world's beauty, holding it through love, empathy, and profound compassion while connecting deeply with human emotions. Point Five gifts you with the power of observation and the ability to discern solutions that might otherwise go unnoticed. At point Six you receive the gift of resilience, enabling you to cultivate the awareness of what is needed to keep us all protected, prepared, and unwavering in the face of adversity. Point Seven brings the gift of optimism, positivity, and spontaneity, infusing even the most challenging tasks with the spirit of joyfulness. Point Eight's gift is leadership, guiding us forward with the purity and strength of an innocent heart, always mindful of keeping our collective well-being intact. Finally, at point Nine, you are blessed with the gift of pure peace, a peace that transcends understanding and can only arise from a heart transformed by light and love.

Imagine that someone has lovingly gifted you with these nine beautifully wrapped presents. Why would you choose to open only one?

In this section, you are encouraged to embark on a journey through all nine Enneagram energies, to explore the connections to your wings, lines, and arrows, as well as the points that may not be part of your primary access. It's important to remember that you always have access to all nine energies, and sometimes, it takes a more deliberate effort to unearth these connections. Embrace this exploration with an open heart, for it's a step toward a deeper understanding of your authentic, multifaceted self, filled with infinite possibilities.

Grounding Meditation

As I move into self-reflection and internal exploration,
I will meditate on these prompts and gently notice
what comes up as I breathe into stillness.

I am ready to begin with three cleansing breaths.

I am inhaling into expansiveness and exhaling constriction.

I have the gift of all nine Enneagram energies within me.

I can freely explore my energy at all nine points.

I am not limited by my type.

I acknowledge my energy and connection to point One and
point Five and utilize them for growth and awareness.

I can freely access my wings at point Six and point Eight.

The Body Center: 8-9-1

In the Body Center, we gain access to our body's wisdom and gut intuition. The Body Center energy is focused on action—affecting the world or environment to avoid being influenced, controlled, or limited by it, and expressing anger or rage in different ways.

What does it look like for me to access
the energies within the Body Center?

Eight

_____

_____

_____

_____

_____

Nine

_____

_____

_____

_____

_____

One

_____

_____

_____

_____

_____

THE HEART CENTER: 2-3-4

In the Heart Center, we gain access to our capacity for emotional honesty and human connection. The Heart Center energy is focused on emotions, self-image, and value—determining your identity and the value you place on your identity plays a key role in how you access the Heart Center energy.

What does it look like for me to access the
energies within the Heart Center?

Two

_____
_____
_____
_____
_____

Three

_____
_____
_____
_____

Four

_____
_____
_____
_____

THE HEAD CENTER: 5-6-7

In the Head Center, we gain access to our ability to reflect, process, and internalize information. The wisdom we have access to in the Head Center energies allows us to cultivate the space we need for objectivity and inner guidance.

What does it look like for me to access the
energies within the Head Center?

Five

_____

_____

_____

_____

_____

Six

_____

_____

_____

_____

_____

Seven

_____

_____

_____

_____

_____

Do I face any challenges connecting to particular
Enneagram energies? Can I explore this further?

Reflecting on the connection to my Six wing, how can Six energy help me stay connected to people and situations and allow me to focus my energy?

_____

_____

_____

_____

_____

_____

_____

_____

_____

_____

_____

_____

_____

_____

_____

_____

_____

_____

_____

The secret to happiness is freedom.

And the secret to freedom is courage.

THUCYDIDES

Reflecting on the connection to my Eight wing, how can Eight energy help me deal with feelings of vulnerability and cultivate the assertiveness I need to become a charismatic and compassionate leader for others?

_____

_____

_____

_____

_____

_____

_____

_____

_____

_____

_____

_____

_____

_____

_____

_____

_____

_____

_____

_____

_____

Embrace your vulnerability and celebrate your flaws; it will let you appreciate the world around you and make you more compassionate.

MASABA GUPTA

At point Seven, I share a connection to point One, which provides an opportunity to explore the gifts and challenges of this energy. On the upside, this energy can help me focus my principled energy and keep me grounded in the present. On the downside, this energy can make me judgmental and dismissive of others. How have I experienced One energy in my life?

_____

_____

_____

_____

_____

_____

_____

_____

_____

_____

_____

_____

_____

_____

_____

_____

_____

_____

We are formed and molded by our thoughts. Those whose minds are shaped by selfless thoughts give joy when they speak or act.

BUDDHA

What does it look like when I tap into the grounded and focused energy at point One? How does my connection to point One affect my actions, behaviors, and beliefs?

_____

_____

_____

_____

_____

_____

_____

_____

_____

_____

_____

_____

_____

_____

_____

_____

_____

_____

_____

_____

_____

I don't have to chase extraordinary moments to find happiness—it's right in front of me if I'm paying attention and practicing gratitude.

BRENÉ BROWN

At point Seven, I share a connection to point Five, which provides an opportunity to explore the gifts and challenges of this energy. On the upside, this energy can bring me the stillness I need to focus my energy to follow through with accountability and find joy in the present. On the downside, this energy can cause me to become detached and cold and limit my ability to connect with others. How have I experienced Five energy in my life?

We must be willing to get rid of the life we've planned, so as to have the life that is waiting for us. The old skin has to be shed before the new one can come.

JOSEPH CAMPBELL

What does it look like when I am able to channel the focus, innovation, and stillness at point Five? How does my connection to point Five affect my actions, behaviors, and beliefs?

_____

_____

_____

_____

_____

_____

_____

_____

_____

_____

_____

_____

_____

_____

_____

_____

_____

_____

_____

When you recover or discover something that nourishes your soul and brings joy, care enough about yourself to make room for it in your life.

JEAN SHINODA BOLEN

Resources for

CONTINUED EXPLORATION

If you would like to continue your Enneagram journey,
we invite you to visit our resources hub at:

DEBORAHEGERTON.COM/RESOURCES

and explore all of the resources we have gathered for you.
This resource hub is updated frequently, so make sure you
check back when you feel the need for a little inspiration.

You are also encouraged to read my books:

*Know Justice Know Peace: A Transformative Journey of Social Justice,
Anti-Racism, and Healing through the Power of the Enneagram*

*Enneagram Made Easy: Explore the Nine Personality Types of the
Enneagram to Open Your Heart, Find Joy, and Discover Your True Self*

**For easy access to the resources hub, use
your smartphone to scan this QR code:**

ABOUT THE AUTHOR

Deborah Threadgill Egerton, Ph.D., is an internationally respected psychotherapist, best-selling author, certified Enneagram teacher, unity and belonging advocate for the healing of humanity, consultant, coach, and spiritual teacher. Dr. Egerton specializes in working with the Enneagram to facilitate intentional change in individuals and organizations.

Affectionately referred to as "Dr. E," she has attained IEA Certification with Distinction for her groundbreaking utilization of the Enneagram in the realm of humanitarian healing. Her work is dedicated to dismantling marginalization and transcending the divisive practice of "othering," offering a guiding path toward the harmonious unification of our global community through the transformative forces of kindness and compassion. Dr. E serves as the president of the International Enneagram Association, the global entity responsible for educating, certifying, and accrediting practitioners, teachers, and schools. In her tenure with the IEA, she has been instrumental in fostering an environment of greater inclusivity and accessibility within the global Enneagram community. Her unwavering commitment to justice, equity, diversity, and inclusion has earned her the affectionate title of "Enneagram JEDI" among her peers.

Dr. E extends her coaching and mentoring expertise to a diverse spectrum of individuals, including best-selling authors, top-tier executives, spiritual luminaries, accomplished therapists, and a myriad of coaches, each hailing from distinct and varied backgrounds. For more than two decades, her work has focused on guiding humanity toward a deeper and more compassionate approach to inner work by harnessing the insights of the Enneagram. Her innovative approach to using the Enneagram in social justice and anti-racism work created a blueprint to reconnect people across all dimensions of diversity and has been implemented in various organizations and entities across the globe. She focuses her work on individuals and organizations to help them release false historical narratives and open their minds and hearts to a more compassionate and connected approach to life.

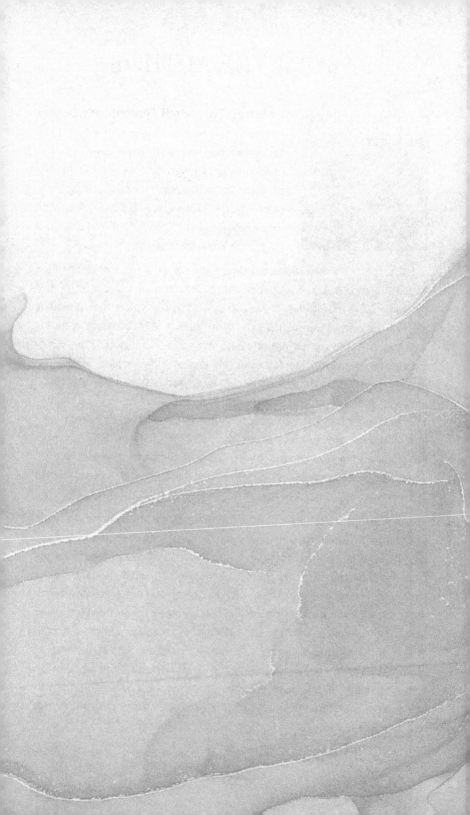

We hope you enjoyed this Hay House book. If you'd like to receive our online catalog featuring additional information on Hay House books and products, or if you'd like to find out more about the Hay Foundation, please contact:

Hay House LLC, P.O. Box 5100, Carlsbad, CA 92018-5100
(760) 431-7695 or (800) 654-5126
www.hayhouse.com® • www.hayfoundation.org

———

Published in Australia by:
Hay House Australia Publishing Pty Ltd
18/36 Ralph St., Alexandria NSW 2015
Phone: +61 (02) 9669 4299
www.hayhouse.com.au

Published in the United Kingdom by:
Hay House UK Ltd
The Sixth Floor, Watson House,
54 Baker Street, London W1U 7BU
Phone: +44 (0) 203 927 7290
www.hayhouse.co.uk

Published in India by:
Hay House Publishers (India) Pvt Ltd
Muskaan Complex, Plot No. 3,
B-2, Vasant Kunj, New Delhi 110 070
Phone: +91 11 41761620
www.hayhouse.co.in

———